# simple machines

# wedges

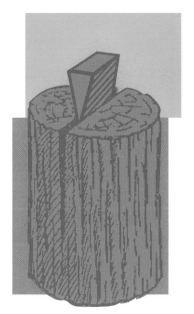

A Buddy Book
by
sarah tieck

ABDO
Publishing Company

# VISIT US AT
### www.abdopublishing.com

Published by ABDO Publishing Company, 4940 Viking Drive, Edina, Minnesota 55435.

Printed in the United States.

Contributing Editor: Michael P. Goecke
Graphic Design: Maria Hosley
Cover Photograph: Photos.com, Clipart.com
Interior Photographs/Illustrations: Clipart.com, Corbis, Photos.com, Professional Litho


## Library of Congress Cataloging-in-Publication Data

Tieck, Sarah, 1976–
   Wedges / Sarah Tieck.
     p. cm. — (Simple machines)
   Includes index.
   ISBN-13: 978-1-59679-816-8
   ISBN-10: 1-59679-816-5
   1. Wedges—Juvenile literature. I. Title. II. Series: Tieck, Sarah, 1976- Simple machines.

TJ1201.W44T54 2006
621.8—dc22

                             2006010045

# Table Of
# Contents

# What Is A Wedge?

Wedges are used to cut, split, pierce, or divide objects. A wedge is a simple machine. A simple machine has few moving parts, sometimes only one.

Simple machines give people a mechanical advantage. This is how wedges help make work easier for people.

A wedge can be used to split a log.

# simple machines

### Inclined Planes
Help move objects.

### Levers
Help lift or move objects.

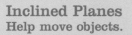

### Pulleys
Help move, lift, and lower objects.

### Screws
Help lift, lower, and fasten objects.

### Wedges
Help fasten or split objects.

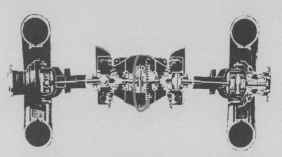

### Wheels and Axles
Help move objects.

Wedges are not the only simple machines. There are six simple machines. These include wedges, levers, pulleys, screws, inclined planes, and wheels and axles.

Sometimes, simple machines work together. Most machines are made up of more than one simple machine. Examples of wedges include forks, nails, and axes.

# Parts of A Wedge

Wedges give people a mechanical advantage. The wedge's design helps open or push objects apart. The wedge can also help people move things such as air and water.

A wedge is usually made up of two inclined planes joined together. The inclined planes make a sharp edge, or point.

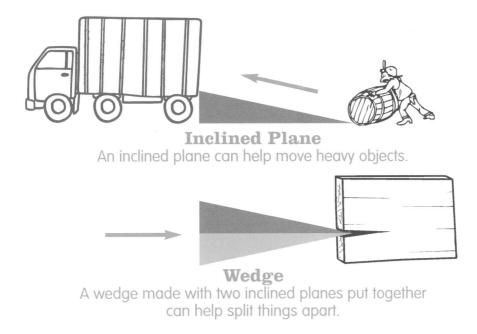

**Inclined Plane**
An inclined plane can help move heavy objects.

**Wedge**
A wedge made with two inclined planes put together
can help split things apart.

The wedge is used to split or move
something. As the wedge cuts through
an object, there is resistance.

Someone or something must supply
force. This force is what makes the
wedge work.

# How Does A Wedge Work?

Most people probably cannot split something solid, such as a log, on their own. But, a person could split a log with a wedge. This is because wedges make work easier.

To use a wedge to split a log, a person could use an ax. He or she would hit the log with the ax's sharp edge.

An ax is one type of wedge.

Downward force helps drive the ax's sharp edge into the log. This creates outward force, splitting the log in two.

# Different Wedges At Work

There are many different ways to use a wedge. It is possible to change a wedge's shape, size, or angle. People can also change the way a wedge moves.

These changes help a wedge to perform different jobs. Because of this, wedges have many uses.

A knife is a wedge. This wedge is narrow, with a sharp edge. By applying downward force to a knife, a person can cut food and other things.

To cut food into pieces, people use a knife as a type of wedge.

Construction workers use nails to build houses and buildings.

Some nails have a wedge, too. This wedge is made up of four inclined planes. By applying downward force with a hammer, the nail's wedge will pierce the wood. This allows the nail to hold the pieces together.

A doorstop is a wedge. It is made of a single inclined plane. By applying sideways force, a person can slide the doorstop under the door. This holds a door open.

An example of a doorstop holding a door open.

A fan blade is a narrow, thin wedge. A motor provides force. As the fan blade turns, it cuts and moves through air.

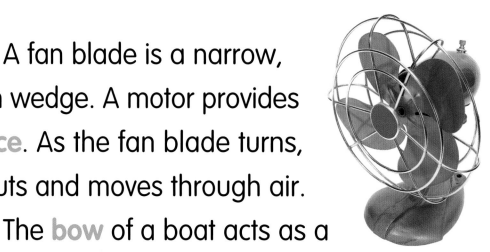

The bow of a boat acts as a wedge. It is a very wide wedge with a dull edge. As the boat moves forward, it pushes apart the water.

The bow of a boat is a wedge that pushes through water.

# The History of Wedges

The wedge has been used for many years. It was one of the first tools and was used by early people.

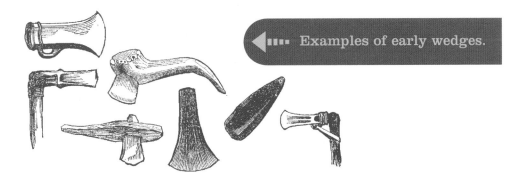

◄···· Examples of early wedges.

A chisel is a useful tool for carving a log into a shape.

In these ancient times, people didn't have machines with motors. They had to do all the work with their bodies.

Ancient peoples made many things by hand. It is said that they used a type of wedge to help remove bark from trees. This tool also helped them make boats from those trees.

# How Do Wedges Help People Today?

Today people have many types of tools but they still use wedges.

When you cut a sandwich with a knife, you are using a wedge. When you use an ice scraper to remove ice from a windshield, you are using a wedge. When you bite into an apple, your teeth are acting as another type of wedge.

Teeth are a type of wedge.
They help people eat their food.

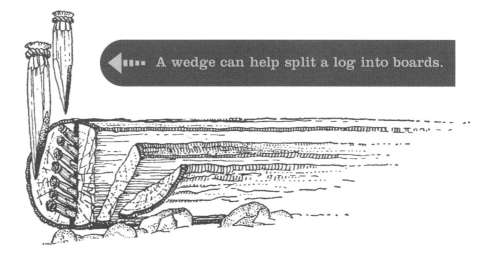

A wedge can help split a log into boards.

Wedges help people with many different jobs all over the world.

# Web Sites

To learn more about **Wedges**, visit ABDO Publishing Company on the World Wide Web. Web site links about **Wedges** are featured on our Book Links page. These links are routinely monitored and updated to provide the most current information available.

### www.abdopublishing.com

# Important Words

angle  the shape made by two straight lines or surfaces meeting in a point.

bow  the front of a boat.

force  a push or pull against resistance.

inclined plane  a flat surface that is raised at one end. This type of simple machine helps move objects to higher or lower places.

mechanical advantage  the way simple machines make work easier. Using a simple machine to help with a task means less, or different, effort is needed to do a job. The same job would require more effort without the help of a simple machine.

resistance  something that works against or opposes.

# Index